Notes from a Desert Place

Notes from a Desert Place

Emily A. Pardue

Kingdom Living Publishing
Accokeek, MD

Cover photograph by Emily A. Pardue

Cover design by TLH Designs, Chicago, IL
www.tlhdesigns.com

Published by
Kingdom Living Publishing
P.O. Box 660
Accokeek, MD 20607
www.kingdomlivingbooks.com

Printed in the United States of America.
ISBN 978-0-9799798-9-7

To the Ravens in My Life

Dr. Ernestine Robinson, Dr. Sharon Marshall, Rev. Anne Henning Byfield, and Rev. Dr. Marion and Clarence Crayton.

Table Of Contents

Introduction

According to Encarta World English Dictionary, desert is an area of land, usually in very hot climates, that consists only of sand, gravel, or rock with little or no vegetation, no permanent bodies of water, and erratic rainfall. It is also a place or situation that is devoid of some desirable thing, or overwhelmed by an undesirable thing. It is a place devoid of life. It is a wild, bleak, and uncultivated place (archaic). Well I can see that; however, it is not devoid of life but it empties you so that you can indeed find life again. For it is in the desert place that you face yourself, and God.

Life is a journey and the exciting thing about this journey is that it is not ours to map out, but it is ours to follow what has been mapped out. I am not writing as one who has already achieved, but one who is encouraging you to continue on the journey. For me this section of my journey has been a time of reflection and pondering. I have learned to let go of bad memories of hurt from people that I cared about and events that were not in my best interest. For a spiritual exercise, I wrote down the names of people that had hurt me and of whom I really had to let go. As I wrote their names, I shaped a blessing for each one by praying for them one by one. This is no new thing. Jesus gave that concept when He said, *". . . bless those who curse you, pray for those who mistreat you"* (Luke 6:28).

I had to let go of those hurts, and of the people who caused the hurt. I giggled as I reflected on each person that caused me pain. I understood they had been searching for what was already available to them. Unfortunately, they could not see that what they needed was right at hand, so they lashed out at anyone, and I appeared to be in their way. It reminded me somewhat of the Wizard of OZ. You know, how the scarecrow longed for a brain but he was already out thinking everyone; how the tin man longed for a heart, yet he was so compassionate; how the lion sought for courage and he was already the bravest. At the end of their journey in OZ, they all found they already possessed what they thought they needed.

While on our journey, many times we find ourselves searching for what we already have. Unlike the OZ journey, often we hurt others along the way. We spend a lot of our time acquiring things or attempting to acquire them, or trying to be someone else, and we do not understand what we can become is already who we are. What we need is being made available to us. It has already been planted in us. It is a part of that being made in God's image (Genesis 1:26). We end up wasting valuable time because we do not get the directions from God, we do not hear the instructions. This leg of my journey has taught me to get the instructions and then follow the directions. It is sad that I am just now getting it, but here I am, and so I proceed to another leg of my journey.

According to Siang-Yang Tan, Brennan Manning gave this benediction at a Pastors Conference:

> May all your expectations be frustrated, all your plans be thwarted, all your dreams be shattered, all your desires be withered into nothingness, so that you may know the powerlessness and poverty of a child, and experience and rest in the love of God the Father, Son, and Holy Spirit, for you (Tan 2006, 104).

That is my prayer for you as you move along the journey. These are my notes left for you to aid in your growth. I encourage you to journal this time. Hear what God is saying to you during this leg of your journey. I bless you with encouragement and peace though each leg of your journey.

Chapter 1

The Journey

I spent entirely too much time trying to format this book and how I thought it should go, especially when Holy Spirit said, "Just write." Well, yes, Holy Spirit does talk, does guide, and if we would listen to Him, as our *Paraclete*, as one who walks along side us, then it would make the journey a little tad simpler and a little less stressful. Jesus promises, *". . . and I will ask the Father, and He will give you another Counselor who will never leave you. He is the Holy Spirit, who leads you into all truth"* (John 14:16-17). The Greek word *Paraclete* means comforter, encourager, and advocate. All of these terms accurately, as best as they can, describe the works of Holy Spirit.

The journey begins because we start. The journey and the route have already been mapped; yet we have a choice. We choose to begin, or we choose to not progress at all. When we begin, we tag on where we come in. We begin by acknowledging that we are on a journey. To understand that this is a journey is itself the beginning of the journey. I do not know the way, but I do know of the journey. The road home is always open. It is never blocked; however, because of our own place and pace in life we may miss the correct path for our progress. That is why we study the road map. In the Scriptures, we see how to go, and what not to do. True, it is not easy; however, the way is made easier when we realize that this is a faith walk. We find that God really is with us and we really can make it, but we must be clear of our faith in God

One way to stay on the path is to watch God. Seek Him and watch what He is doing in your life. There are times that you must step back or step outside of how you function. You do it just to get a glimpse of what God sees. He will allow you to see yourself and you just may find you are not as bad as you thought, yet you are not as good as you can be. You need direction, and that is where Holy Spirit comes in.

Oh the way—at one point it appeared that everything I had ever hoped for was right there, right in my reach. Have you ever been there? In one vision, I found myself with everything right within my grasp. You know how you do when you think that this is it, all is well, and the world is just rosy? I thought that this was finally it! God said, "Don't." There I was standing on a cliff, everything I wanted was in reach, and God said, "Don't reach. Watch with me." So I stood there with Him and then suddenly I was no longer on the cliff but floating downward and everything was floating upward passing me by. I was fine, yet I did not understand what was happening. It was all right there for me, yet I could not reach for it. I could not say anything. It was indeed a safe place for me but everything I thought was mine was floating past me out of my reach. God said, "Don't reach. Watch with Me." I thought, 'Others are expecting this of me.' But God said, "Don't reach. Watch with Me." So what could I do with that vision? You know how we act when we do not understand something, don't you? We make excuses for events that do not happen as we had envisioned, or as we had shared with others. I watched what I thought was to be mine fade away. Oh, I heard the remarks of others as they jeered, "Hmp—I thought so. She is not all that." But it was never mine to make excuses for what did not happen. I learned not to share everything with everyone, even in the church. Everyone who walks in your area may not be walking alongside you. In spite of that, there is a place where we must believe what God has said and we must obey.

Now, over two years later, I am beginning to understand that scene better. While we can reach for the sky, we must be careful not to overreach for the counterfeit. Many times, we reach beyond what God has for us, because what God has does not appear to be large enough, rich enough, or as spectacular as we think it should. It may not be big enough—a church that is large enough, friends who are good enough, associates who have enough influences. If we make unwise decisions, we will lose what we have already been given. Wise decisions involve listening and obeying God and we will receive what belongs to us.

What I saw was not mine to have at that time; it was just not mine. We have heard the cliché, "What God has for me is for me;" that is true. Too often, we chase the wrong thing, which causes us to miss the right thing. You fill in the blank for the thing you chase: fame, success, money, men, women, etc. You get the picture? These things are as fleeting as they are temporal. Integrity, honor, and faith should be our goal. Can you see the difference? The passage in Matthew gives us a foundation: *"But seek first His kingdom and His righteousness, and all these things will be given to you as well"* (Matthew 6:33). When we strive to do that, then we can rest in watching God's move in our life. Had I reached out to grab the counterfeit, I would have never achieved all that God has for me. So I watched. And I still wait.

It appears that God moved everything that I was accustomed to out of my way. I know that it is right there. Just right there, but I cannot touch it. I cannot see it. Why? It is like being in the dark. The dark is frightening; yet when I stop crying and listen, I can hear Him, I can feel Him. I know that I am not alone and my way is made clear. This is not something I heard or read about, it is something I know. I cannot find hope in anyone else, in anything else; believe me, I tried. My only hope is in God. Why is it so difficult for us to hope in God? Oh, we talk a good game, but no one wants to really deal with it. Oh but in that hope—we have a stand. God is teaching me how to move with my physical eyes closed and my spiritual eyes on Him alone. You could say, "Walking with my eyes shut wide open." That can only be done through the guidance of Holy Spirit.

I do not know if I would invite anyone into this leg of the journey. When I was in seminary and I read of the trials the spiritual mothers, fathers, and writers experienced. While intriguing as the sharing of their 'desert place' was, I did not want to go through anything like that. Sure, it prepared them for what they would do, but surely, I could go a different way. I wanted so bad to take the journey, but without the pain. There are so many different legs of the journey. I remember once sharing with Rev.

Johnnie Green, my late pastor's assistant. We were in his office a few months after Doc had died and I announced that I was on a journey and I didn't know where it would take me, but when I left I would come back and tell him I was gone. Rev. Green looked at me and said, "Yeah. He explained that he and Doc had talked about the time when I would have to leave Tabernacle. It was part of my journey. I told him that I knew I was on a journey but now, instead of being pulled, I was gently nudged by Holy Spirit along my way. I was now aware and making steps myself. That was then, it was difficult enough as it took me away from what I knew, and I so wanted to do "good" so I would not have to meet the 'desert place.'

Here I am in the 'desert place,' in this leg of my journey, and it has released me from all other connections. This place follows God on a quest that shows Him to be so real time and time again. It is scary! If I invite others, they would blame me for their heartache and I really cannot handle too much more of others' blame. "Lord, it is a journey and I know that you would not have brought me along if I couldn't handle it. Let me feel you. Let me hear you. Then let me rest on your love. Let me rest in your care."

Wow! I am here. I have finally entered a place where being lonely is no longer a concern; where lack of husband is no longer a concern; where what the others have done to me and have tried to do to me is no longer a concern. They could not succeed in destroying me because God has kept me. I could not even succeed inadvertently in destroying myself because God has kept me. This is a place where none of the temporal matters anymore. It is difficult for others who are looking in to understand. They think

I should act like, be like, do like, what they think is God's will for my life, or at least for the status quo. But 'they' can't understand my time in this place. It is a place of refining, of restoring, of re-equipping. This is a place of restructuring my heart and my walk. It is my renewal by God. "So Father, how do I write? Do I write to them, for them? Or to You -for them? Or for me alone? Show me what You want."

One day, while talking with my sister Terry, I had another vision. There was a large white house with a long wrap-around porch and a swing on the porch. The front door was open, inviting me in. The path of my journey would take me through this house. Peering inside the house from the porch, all I could see was darkness. It was so dark that it was frightening, yet I knew I had to go in. I longed to go in, but I paused. I looked back off the porch. In the yard were preachers laughing at me for going on the porch. They were having a good time among themselves, but I had distracted them. Going on the porch did not appeal to them, much less entering the house. They joked about my urge to go in, about my wanting to be different. They said I could not know what was best because I did not have enough experience in matters as they did. I did not want to leave the porch to join them. I wanted to go in. I knew my way was through the dark house. I did not know how many rooms were dark, or how long it would take to get through the house, but I had to go in.

After I shared this vision, Terry warned me to be careful not to look down my nose at those in the yard who wanted to stay outside and play. I understood that. If what God has for me is through the darkness, I will go. That has been a grand place of challenge for me as I take the road less traveled. That road leads through trials and dangers yet I do not go alone. Others choose not to take the road, not to venture to the porch, much less go into the darkness. They choose to stay outside, and that is fine. I answered that those who choose to stay outside laugh at me and wonder what I will do next and how will I make it. We must have something to hold on to and one of my Scriptures is one that my son Marq loves also:

> *But as for me, I watch in hope for the Lord. I wait for God my Savior; my Go will hear me. Though I have fallen, I will rise. Though I sit in darkness, the Lord will be my light. Because I have sinned against Him, I will bear the Lord's wrath, until He pleads my case and establishes my right. He will bring me out into the light; I will see His righteousness. Then my enemy will see it and will be covered with shame, she who said to me, "Where is the Lord your God?"* (Micah 7:7-10)

It depends on the choices you make. You can choose to stay outside or choose to follow what God has for you. Yes, someone must stay out in the yard, but there are so many other ventures waiting, if you will follow God's lead.

In another vision, I was going down a stairway and a woman—a dancer—was in my way. This was significant because I developed and directed liturgical dancers and I knew she was a liturgical dancer. "Liturgical dance ushers people into the presence of the Lord, and He takes it from there" (Pardue 2005,

14). The liturgical dancer blocking my way was eye opening. She was the one that I had to go around on my way down. There were sprinklings of people going up, but the dancer was blocking me from going down. Then the Lord showed me that I was on the same path with a lot of people that I had nothing in common with except we were all going down. I cried out, "No! Am I going to hell?" He answered, "No," then I understood. Those going down were following the desires, the dreams of others for their lives. Those going up were using their gifts, their talents for God's purpose. The dancer was a warning for me somewhat like Balaam's donkey in the twenty-second chapter of Numbers. Just like Balaam, after inquiring of the Lord and receiving instructions, Balaam was swayed by others and inquired of God again. The Lord had already given me direction; yet, I inquired many times more because others thought I was to do something else. You know how a child keeps begging for something until they get it? I kept asking because, "Surely others know better about my life than I do." Now you know, I did not believe that but that is how I acted. That is how you act also.

When Balaam's way was blocked by his donkey three times, he beat her. After the third time the Lord let the donkey speak. The donkey was trying to save Balaam's life from an angel sent to kill him. I have always loved that story and now here I am at that road, on a stairway. The dancer was sent to block me from turning on my gifts, my talents and following others in what they thought was best for me. The dancer was on that stairway to block me from aborting my mission by giving up on myself. I cried out, "Lord help me to go up! I don't want to follow others' dream for my life."

That vision came at a pivotal moment. At some point, after becoming so discouraged, I had begun to listen to others on what I was to do in my life. I felt a failure and felt myself giving up. It is so easy to get off track of what God has for you. The sad part is that I teach others to stay on track, by listening to the guidance of the Holy Spirit. What is it about us that can cause us to be distracted so easily? Why do we so quickly forget that the journey will take us through some things? There will be some hard spots and some fun ones. There will be some detours, but we must not get lost on them. The journey through these periods shapes us into more of who we are. Yes, it hurts, but we do not complain when all is well, do we? It is a journey and process of perfecting us. We cannot perfect ourselves; the Holy Spirit knows what we need to be perfected. We just need to listen to the guidance and watch what God does with us. Too often, we watch what is happening to others and we miss our own perfecting by God.

We are all different, our journeys are different; our levels of understanding are different. We should celebrate those differences by learning from one another. No one person holds all the answers; together we help one another. That is how the community of believers flourishes—through loving and helping, praying and encouraging, supporting and protecting. When we become so rigid in what we think, we may break at some point. I like how Francois Fenelon, a Catholic Bishop prayed together with a Protestant that was dying, "Thou knowest, my Savior, that I desire to live and die in the Truth; forgive me if I was mistaken" (Fenelon 1992, iv). Let us long to live and die in the truth, and let us appreciate others who have the same desire.

You will be surprised that the more you see through with your spiritual sight, the more you can celebrate as God's created.

I love traveling. I love to see God's wonders in other places. I love the plants, the way of life, and the people. God created it all and we should celebrate that. You do not have to travel to do that, it just helps to give you a better picture of your small but significant spot in life. It is a spot well worth celebrating; that is a significant part of the journey. Do not miss what God has for you on this journey.

Chapter 2

To Follow

We say that we have discovered our purpose and that we recognize our ministry. The idea, "to have a ministry," is so misused. Many people want to brag about "their ministry." Sadly, we call them "wanna-be's." That is our inside joke, but what they do not realize is that every believer has an assignment and every believer is already 'somebody' to God. Ministry does not start or stop at the church door. Ministry calls for a special level of commitment and obedience. You must discover your purpose. Find what God has for you. *"What anyone else dares to boast about—I am speaking as a fool—I also dare to boast about"* (2 Corinthians 11:21b). That is Paul's boast. Unfortunately, many times, our boast is not like Paul. We all want the glory without the pain, but in this passage in verses 23-33, Paul breaks it down in what he has already gone through:

Five times beaten, thirty-nine lashes, three times beaten with rods, once stoned, three times shipwrecked—day and night spent in open sea; constantly on the move, dangers from rivers, bandits, from own countrymen, Gentiles, in the city, in the country, danger at sea, danger from false brothers; labored and toiled—gone without sleep, known hunger and thirst, cold and naked.

That is a lot to handle. There is a southern saying that works better when you see accompanying picture. It is of an old hound dog lazily lying on the porch watching the younger dogs race by. The saying: "If you can't run with the big dogs, stay on the porch." Let me flip that. Why do we think we are doing the Kingdom such a great favor? Our suffering is not like Paul, yet we are in the race. However, let us not get too caught up, because —hey, Paul is a big dog. Can we follow Paul's example for the Kingdom? Oh, do not say it. It may not be required, even more may be required. No one knows what is required of them until they are at that position. So what can we say? What is required? *"He has shown you what is good. And what does the Lord require of you? To act justly, and to love mercy, and to walk humbly with your God"* (Micah 6:8). In following God, we can indeed succeed. It may not be as we want, yet it is part of our journey.

Do we really understand our purpose? God has a divine plan and part of that plan involves watching and following Him. The journey is exciting because we cannot map it out; we follow what has been mapped out. This mapping out is something akin to following the yellow brick road in the Wizard of Oz. Where are we going? We are on our way home. We start out in order to get home. If we keep that thought in perspective, it will help when we feel we may have lost the way. It will get scary and confusing sometimes. Probably the hardest thing is not being aware that you are going the wrong way. Has that ever happened to you?

There will be times that you may be positively sure that you are going right and it will be so not right. Now the next statement may be difficult for some, as some guys I have been around do not like to ask for directions. That is not sexist, for some reason they just do not ask. We all must learn to stop and ask for directions, and then follow them. That may be the reason that so many of us get off track. The Psalmist says, *"Guide my steps by Your Word, so I will not be overcome by evil"* (Psalm 119:132 NLT).

We must get direction and no one can guide but Holy Spirit, who will stand with you through the encounters along the way. Holy Spirit can guide you safely through, around, or over any obstacles. It is all a part of following the leader. So, what is so great in following the leader? When we were young, I loved the game. I loved both following and leading. I would follow others while thinking up better ways to lead. While leading I was pleasantly surprised that others had thoughts about things I had missed. So it works both ways.

It was then I realized that I thought 'outside the box.' Many things I thought about or saw I could not tell others, but incorporated into my leadership skills. I could see or feel an obstacle and steer around it while others never saw the obstacle. Even then, I had to be careful not to let my skills or my gifts get the best of me.

Terry and I were talking about a problem that a friend from Ethiopia was having. I shared with that friend what was happening in her situation and suggested to her a solution. She could not see it and it took her a while to absorb the suggestion. Later I remarked that I did not understand why our friend could not see the solution. Terry responded, "Many people cannot think and see what you see, and you need to help them see." That took a while to sink in. I had to learn to use my gifts for the good.

Over the years, I have used my gifts to fight union causes by arguing for others who could not speak for themselves, for those who had lost their "voice" or had never found their "voice." At times I abused my gifts and talents and misrepresented God. But when I got on track I began to help others. It is all a part of the journey. It has become clear that I do not have to do anything but what has been laid out for me by God. God points me toward others and situations for my benefit as well as for their benefit. If the situation is missed in that moment through mistaken ideas—oh well. It is our loss. I do not want to lose any more opportunities. How about you?

Most of the time you need to get still to find the way. At times you may be silenced in order to hear from God. At all times you must remember who is providing guidance on this journey. It is not another person, and it is not you. Jesus assured the disciples:

If you love Me, you will obey what I command. And I will ask the Father, and He will give you another Counselor to be with you forever- The Spirit of Truth. The world cannot accept Him, because it neither sees Him nor knows Him. But you know Him, for He lives with you, and will be in you. I will not leave you as orphans; I will come to you (John 14:15-18).

Where am I going with this? Our gifts are to be used to advance the Kingdom of God, and we must be careful not to misuse them. I have seen too many leaders in the church who abuse their gifts and abuse their congregation. Instead of freeing the congregants to become strong disciples, they cripple them as broken servants. And they hold over these broken people the passage, *"Touch not Mine anointed, and do My prophets no harm"* (1 Chronicles 16:22 KJV). They arbitrarily use that passage as their "get out of jail free" card. They misuse the congregation through unfounded power, misplaced sex, and want of money. Many of their members are broken from that spiritual abuse by the very ones who are to protect them. They are too afraid to speak up because of that passage. And these abusive leaders will also hurt other leaders who choose to speak out against this type of abuse. I was told a few times by different ones that some pastors wanted to destroy me. Isn't that hilarious? Oh that mere man could destroy God's doing! Okay, okay. How can we get back on track? As followers, we must be careful who we follow, and as leaders we must take care how we lead. For example, Twitter is the buzz to follow others with tweets of information, and to allow others to follow what you are doing. Yes, I am on Twitter but I believe the responsibility remains the same. Be careful.

As Jesus preached that day on the mountainside in Galilee, Luke says that the crowds surrounded Jesus and His disciples. They came from all over Judea, Jerusalem, servants of Tyre and Sidon. They came from many miles to hear Jesus, and they came to be healed. Everyone tried to touch Him because healing power went out (Luke 6:17-19). See it in the passage. The people are there to see Jesus. Don't get it confused. They are there to hear

27

and to be in the presence of Jesus, not to hear the disciples.

I had a seminary student question my use of a book for a course the student needed. That was troubling enough. Then, in a paper, he questioned the exegetical content of another author while his own thoughts on the lesson were quite muddled. Isn't that so like us? We do not know a subject, yet we are quick to criticize; but isn't that how we do God? You see, asking questions allow us to learn, but 'questioning' may set us up for confusion. Often, 'questioning' says we believe we have answers and want to assert our intelligence over another. It's a game that people play. How can the one created question the creator? Sometimes our critical ideas can cause us to forget who we are following on the journey.

The gospels record Jesus' Sermon on the Mount. That day on the hill, people were healed; they were delivered at that gathering. If people were being healed by Jesus, then why is it not done now? Jesus is the same yesterday, today, and forever. In our gatherings as church, "Why are people not being healed?" Why can they not recognize His touch? Can you recognize His touch? Why are we, as preachers, not pointing others to the source of our peace, of our salvation? When do we follow Jesus' example? When do we help others find their way to Jesus? Where is our power? Could it be that we have missed Jesus as the source of our peace and our salvation? Could it be that we have not experienced the true joy of Jesus? Surely that must be it, because we would want others to experience that freedom in salvation. Could it be that we have abused our responsibility of leading others and refused our responsibility to follow Jesus?

Chapter 3

The Pause

Along this journey, there are pauses on roadblocks, and obstacles around the path. The path is still there, but we have to find it. Pauses can come in many ways. There are times you may believe that God is nowhere near you; yet somehow that appears to be the time when God is right there, so close watching, protecting, and hovering over like a mother hen. I have had my share of pauses on my journey. One major pause for me lately was with my sister's health.

When I got the call that Terry's heart rate was very low and no one knew why. . . . Wow! What can you say? What would cause something so perfectly made by God to not cooperate with His divine will? The Psalmist praises, *"I will praise You because I am fearfully and wonderfully made; Your works are wonderful, I know that well"* (Psalm 139:14). What would cause an otherwise perfectly working heart to slow down and not beat to God's will? How do we respond to something of that magnitude? We are promised life, yet we miss how precious that life is, to us and to God. How can we praise God while in our pause? That is when praise is needed. Praise will bring you to a place of peace in the pause. At times, God will place you in a pause and while in that pause the best you can do is hear from Him.

I have come to realize that the pauses in my life assist me in taking a self-inventory. There are times that I need to take a moment to look around, to measure where I am, and to gain a better understanding of what God would have of me. It is so easy to go off down a track of noble cause, which has nothing at all to do with our particular journey. Terry's illness was indeed a pause moment. It brought me back to reality that life is so very precious and so very short; and family is all we have. It was a time for letting go, and it was not easy. I had to let go in order to trust that God had Terry's life under control. And look at what He did with her! She is fine now and continues to honor God with her life.

I believe detours are the most encountered obstacles along this journey. Detours take us off track; they cause us to go around, to take a different route. Many times they are an inconvenience to us, but they can mess us up. Detours take us away from what we know, from what is safe. Lack of the core longings of safety, worth, value, love, nurture, encouragement, appreciation, and God can cause us to detour.

On one of my many trips to seminary in Ohio I found myself detoured on a road that I had never seen before. The detour was so long that I began to worry that I had missed the signs back to my main route. Now, I had been on the phone talking the whole time. I got off the phone and began to watch for signs. Then the Lord showed me not to panic but enjoy the sights as they belonged to Him, and learn from them. Farther down the road I was back on course. What did I learn from this? Don't get lost on the detour, stay the course. Sometimes detours are for our benefit, just to get us back on course. Millicent Thompson wrote a few years ago, *"Don't Die in the Winter: Your Season is Coming"* (Thompson 1995). Detours happen, don't get lost on them.

A major detour for me that shook my life was loss of financial stability. It took quite a while before I realized that it was only God and me in that place. Had my heart and eyes been open I would have realized sooner. Instead I got caught up in my own hurt and missed God's work in my life. It was the desert place.

What can you do when nothing you do works? What do you do when you have done all you can? Have you ever been there? You know, when nothing works and things that should bring you some kind of financial support brings nothing. And you get deeper in debt with no way out? Even those in the church will not come to your aid, and you are surprised by those who do come? Have you been there when people treat you like a leper, and whisper gossip about you? I had never been in this place before, a place where nothing I did worked for me and everyone thought I should have been doing everything. You are knocked down by some force and people are standing around insisting that you get up. However, you can't get up; yet here I was in that place and Donnie McClurkin answered the question, "What do you do when you've done all you can?" Stand! It took a while to get to the place to hear God. I was too busy wondering 'how it happened' and 'what to do next.' When God asked, "Are you crying because you are with Me?" That was my 'wake up.' That is when I begin to see where I was. The desert place is a major pause.

What did that episode mean to me? Oh so many lessons. I do understand that 'it is not about me.' It never was. What we go through is not about us, but serves to aid others on the journey. Oh yeah, it is hard, but each day brings new revelations. I have learned not to fret. Sure, I long for a time when I am financially stable again. But you know, I am still who I am. I awake each day with awe in knowing that this is another day to behold God's mercies. You can choose to awaken each morning to explore the wonders of God's hand, or not. Each new day there are so many ways to make a difference in another's life, and that makes a difference in your life. We should strive to make a positive difference. This journey is ours to take alone but we make it while moving in and out of the journeys of others. Think about how many people you come in contact with everyday. You can make a profound difference by a smile, a prayer for someone. No, they do not need to know that you are praying for them. Identify at least one person everyday and pray for their well being. You do not need to know their story; Holy Spirit will show you what to pray. Look around you. Think how another's life episodes may be tied to you. Search for an answer to the connection. Get outside of yourself and you will find a stronger connection to your brother, your sister.

Pause—Hmmm. Just to stop our constant motion is quite difficult. Even when we physically stop, our minds continue to race on. Slow down; focus on an object—a picture, a flower, a scene, anything serene. Then explore that serene place, search for God, enjoy His wonders in that serenity. Pause. . . hear the joy of that pause . . . rest. . . trust God in that place. "The point of trusting God is not to do great things that you can feel good about, but to trust God from a place of deep weakness" (Fenelon 1992, 66). The pause gives you a place to explore yourself in order to trust God.

Chapter 4

Too Much Baggage

When you strive to follow God, at times you may feel a binding, a stifling, a hindrance from moving forward. You could be spiritually bound. That bondage can develop under so many guises. What trips you up may not be what you think is tripping you. Every Biblical character that God used had flaws. They all had people, places, and things that tripped them up or lured them into a not-so-perfect position. And it is that way with us. We are not perfect, yet God uses us as imperfect vessels to do a perfect mission. He uses us, many times to our breaking point, to do His will. I think this breaking point may be the best place we need to be in order to effectively follow His will. It is not easy but it is achievable.

It is time to stop and ponder; examine what may be holding you from following God's will for your life. Then strive to leave that hindrance. It is not easy, but I promise, it can be done. You leave it by walking towards God's will. It is so much easier to walk toward something than to walk from anything. Walking away keeps you focused on what you are leaving. However, when you focus on moving toward, then you can let go of what is behind. Jesus said, *"Anyone who puts a hand to the plow and looks back is not fit for the kingdom"* (Luke 9:62 NLT). Looking back will keep you back.

The walk forward is in steps, but you can do it. There are only two steps that really count. Let me give you what I learned about the journey. I learned from hearing about the Olympic torch from a professor, colleague, prayer warrior, and friend, Dr. Walter Kime. It has such a profound effect on me that I refer to it often, with my commentary of course. He had a chance to participate in the carrying of the Olympic torch as it made its way through Ohio. This is my take on hearing from Walt. I call it, "The Race We Run."

The Race We Run

There are many torches, or vessels, for carrying the flame. We carry the torch, not the flame. We can hold the torch, but we cannot hold the flame. We can polish the torch but we cannot touch the flame. We can extinguish it, but we cannot hold it. The flame is the Holy Spirit. It is the Holy Spirit that ignites mankind's heart. The church is the vessel that helps to carry the flame. It is the Holy Spirit that causes people to change, not the church. We can carry the torch, not the flame. God asked Jeremiah, *"Is not My Word like fire, and a hammer that breaks a rock to pieces?"* (Jeremiah 23:29).

Over 11,000 candidates applied for the honor of carrying the torch in Ohio alone, yet only one was chosen, and that was Walt. While so many events, so many ideas, appear to be pushing ahead of you, what God has for you is for you. Remain faithful and watch what God does. Nothing can take what belongs to you.

There were so many volunteers who took time off from their jobs, who were committed to aid the one carrying the torch. You do not know who God has already placed in your path just to aid you along, or to run interference for you along this leg of your journey.

As Walt practiced and practiced, he watched everything going on around him; that is when he discovered the Olympic spirit. You do not run to win; you run to finish! Look at that another way. Wouldn't that be a load off your mind if you fully understood that God is not waiting for you at the end with a stopwatch? You do not have anyone you need to beat, but just to finish this race.

I don't mean to say that I have already achieved these things or that I have already reached perfection! Yet I keep working toward that day when I will finally be all that Christ Jesus saved me for and wants me to be. No, dear brothers and sisters, I am still not all I should be, but I am focusing all my energies on this one thing: Forgetting the past and looking forward to what lies ahead, I strain to reach the end of the race and receive the prize for which God, through Christ Jesus, is calling us up to heaven (Philippians 2:12-14 NLT).

The Olympic officials gave Walt the choice, to run, walk, or go in a wheelchair. He chose to run. We have the option on how we run this race; run or walk, the race is ours to complete. Paul attests to Jesus' favor, *"My gracious favor is all you need. My power works best in your weakness"* (2 Corinthians 12:9b).

We do not always get what we want in this race, and I'm sure that is a good thing. Walt had prayed that the leg of his run would not be at night, it was. He prayed that his race would not be uphill, it was. God blesses us with what we need and not always what we want. Most of the time we do not understand what we are asking, and we ask amiss. To remedy praying amiss, I endorse praying God's divine will for your life. With you in agreement with God's will in any situation, you cannot go wrong. As Walt began his nighttime, uphill race, he could only see the faces of those gathered to cheer him on. He saw his wife, his grandchildren, and strangers all there to encourage the one who carries the torch.

Therefore, since we are surrounded by such a great cloud of witnesses, let us throw off everything that hinders and the sin that so easily entangles, and let us run with perseverance, the race marked out for us. Let us fix our eyes on Jesus, the author and perfecter of our faith, who for the joy set before him endured the cross, scorning its shame, and sat down at the right hand of the throne of God. Consider him who endured such opposition from sinful men, so that you will not grow weary and lose heart (Hebrews 12:1-3).

As Walt prepared for the handoff, the torch of the one running was about a foot apart from Walt's torch, yet the flame leaped from one torch to the other torch! The flame leaped into his torch. He was waiting for the hand off. Why is that so significant? The flame can be passed on, but we cannot catch the flame unless we are in waiting mode; then we can receive. The Holy Spirit ignites us and we can take off.

Walt remembered two steps in the race. When he received the flame, he was gone! The only two steps he remembered were the first step and the last step. Those are the only two that are most important in life: the first, that you start the race and the last, that you finish the race. The middle steps are not as important if you are allowing Holy Spirit to lead. Do not worry about the middle steps; God has already worked them out. The Word says, *"Direct my footsteps according to your Word; let no sin rule over me"* (Psalm 119:133).

We carry something very precious in this race as vessels of the flame. Often we have more than we need to carry—too much baggage. We lose our way with too much baggage. We cannot hear our directions when we carry too much baggage. Please understand that the most important thing we carry is the flame of the Holy Spirit. We can run knowing that nothing can deter us from what God has for us. We may not understand but we can be assured that God has already placed those running interference for us. We do not run this race to win, but to finish. There are those who have gone before us who bear witness to the grace of God that they made it and we will too. There are only two steps that matter, the first and the last. We run expecting Holy Spirit in communion. The first step has been taken; run until you hear, *"Well done, good and faithful servant."*

Chapter 5

Not Smart

This place in my life thrust me into a place that I have never been before. It was so financially detrimental that all I could do was cry most of the time. I still ministered to others, but when I got alone, I would cry. I had my buy-out from my job which was to last me quite a few years. I did quite a bit of remodeling. I thought I was doing a good thing and paid for the work out of my money in order not to make another bill. I learned that was terribly not smart. That was one of a few 'not smart' moves. How many times have we made 'not smart' moves believing them to be smart? Unfortunately, we have few people that we can receive good advice from and so we suffer. We are overly cautious because we do not know whom we can trust. In "loving one another," we should be able to find a safe place in the community of believers: *"By this all men will know that you are my disciples, if you love one another"* (John 13:34).

Speaking of 'not smart,' I was playing a game with my son and his family. The oldest grandson, Adonis, 14 years (at that time), was misleading the middle grandson, Trey, who was eight. They were peeking at one another's hand and both were working to help Adonis win while the Trey got further from winning.

You could see them plotting against everyone yet Adonis was still winning, and Trey was still losing. The youngest grandson, Adam, then six, could even see what was happening. My daughter-in-law, Cathy, and I both told Adonis and Trey to stop playing as they were. They kept it up, I could not take it any longer and I told Trey that what he was doing was not smart. Later after the game was over and Adonis had won, Trey said to me, "Grandma Nette, you said I was stupid." I corrected him and explained, "'Not smart' does not mean that you are stupid. It means that you are not thinking things through." Then we rehearsed the events as they unfolded in the game. Trey is a very bright and creative boy but during that game he played, "not smart." The 'not smarts' can get anyone. We are vulnerable to them but in a community of believers there should be those that will warn against the 'not smarts.' That is an ingredient of loving one another.

Often we play 'not smart' in life. I played 'not smart' financially and, with the stock market wrecking havoc a few times, I lost. With no income, it was indeed a different place for me. So, I made a terribly 'not smart' move by accepting a position at a church plant (which proved to be a hoax). By not waiting on God, I had taken the position for money and ministry. Although there was ministry, I went for the wrong reason. (See how easily we can get off track?) I appeared to be heading downward. For at least a month and a half, I cried every day. I felt useless, worthless, a failure, with my saved, sanctified, degreed self. I threw major pity parties for the only ones that showed up—me, myself and I. With those three, I had no need of anyone else, so I shut out the Father, the Son, and Holy Spirit. Oh yeah, I cried to God, but I did not want to hear His reply. I was too busy in pity. I was afraid to take directions from the Holy Spirit as I had already made too many wrong moves. I questioned everything. All I could see was me losing everything and with no place to go. The shame! "Oh woe is me." Can you see it? Pity parties are usually hosted by vanity; and pride will take you down.

I was so worried about all that I was going through. I understood that I was in a desert place, yet I still wanted to fix it all from where I was. I had heard and read of the 'desert place' experience. John of the Cross calls it the 'dark night of the soul.' I greatly admired those who went through it, though; I would have preferred to bypass it. After all, hadn't I already gone through enough? You know how we are? We want the prize without the sweat equity. I had read all about it, so I knew from their experiences. I did not learn, I just read about their experiences. I knew they had gone through much, but I could not learn from their experiences. My mother used to say, "Experience is a good teacher." I did not want that experience. I wanted to "be good;" I did not want to go through. You see I knew the 'desert place' to be a learning place, but I understood it to be a place of punishment. After all, what was God working out in all the spiritual writers and church fathers and mothers? I have learned, while it may feel like punishment, it is a perfecting to get the best out of self. To experience it for one's self is indeed eye opening and heart searching. Do you know what to do when God has you in a desert place? You wait. You do not move or think away from that place, or outside of that place. You really cannot do anything but wait and watch God. You really have to focus on where you are and whom you are with in that place. Here is the most difficult part: God may respond, or He may not for a time, but ultimately He will respond. The desert place is one of facing your biggest challenges, yourself. It is where you get a glimpse of yourself, who you really are, and of what you were created to do.

I began to see the wasted, useless ways that I handled so many things. I had to take care not to fall into another pity party of what I had done, or what I could have done, you know of wasted time. There are so many challenges in the desert. I suppose the Lord got tired of my crying and one day He asked, "Are you crying because you are with Me?" That was when I begin to stop struggling. It took another month before I could look around and see where I was. Yes, I was in a desert place, but I was not alone. No, I could not see Him, but I was aware that He was there. So I tried to see what I was to see. I was not smart enough to understand where I was, so I struggled.

Sometimes we struggle against God and miss the plans that He has for us. If you think the desert place was easy, it was not; it was hard, it was lonely, it was indescribable, and it was where I do not care to be ever again. No one could really hear me; no one could even answer my questions. I could not get a job. I tried, but I could not get one. You see that is what I thought I needed, but I needed more. I needed Jesus. I needed to be still and to hear. Then I began to respond to my suggestions that I once asked of those who struggled. "Well, can't she do something?" "She could leave some things off her resume in order to get something." "She could get a job somewhere even if it is not what she wanted." "I mean, even for a while, couldn't she?" "No, she couldn't." I had the answer; when God closes the doors nothing is available to you until He opens them. All I could do was wait. I began to hear clearer, and through tears, through my pain, I began to rely on God.

You see, that is the thing. We say it, but we really do not understand what it means to rely on God. Relying on God means not having a plan B. He is the plan. There I was in that place, friends could not understand and offered solutions for me from repenting to trying harder to listening more. That was extremely difficult as my whole life was being consumed by looking for a job. There was no money, lack of teaching opportunities, and lack of paid ministry opportunities. Even when God said, "Be still," I would stop looking for employment for an hour or two, and then I would panic and start looking again, so that people would see I was trying. In disobeying God, I had forgotten one small thing: "You cannot outrun God." If you try, that is definitely not smart. Not smart is depending on yourself, and not relying on God. Not smart is following friends' advice and dreams for you, and not living your own dreams.

I could not understand. Don't think it has been easy, but I could breathe a little easier knowing that it was His plan for me. Just like He did with Elijah, God allowed the ravens to feed me. *"So he did what the Lord had told him. He went to the Kerith Ravine, east of the Jordan, and stayed there. The ravens brought him bread and meat in the evening, and he drank from the brook"* (1 Kings 17:5-6). Elijah did not go hungry. He was obedient to God, and God provided for him. Do you know how small a raven's beak is? It may have taken a few flights or many ravens, yet the ravens fed Elijah as God commissioned. Elijah lived, and so I am living proof that God will care for His own. That is definitely smart.

Chapter 6

Theory of 'I Don't Know'

When you are in the desert place, you may begin to understand that the way is not clear, and the path is not straight. I have finally come to an understanding that I just do not know. In my desert place, I called my sister and told her, "I don't know" and she said, "Now you are where God wants you." So from this place of 'I don't know,' I can say, "When you think you have all the answers; when you think you know what you are to do in ministry; when you think you know your part of God's work; you will do strange things that take you farther away from your purpose." You take God by the hand and say, "Come bless what I am doing for You." Yes, that is what you do. However, when you do not know . . . when you acknowledge that you have no clue, then you can ask for the way. Jesus said that He was "the way, the truth and the life" (John 14:6). When you do not know, you can seek direction from Holy Spirit. You are here for God's purpose. You do not know what that is, but you will be guided when you ask.

When you think you know, you accept so much responsibility that was never yours. A while ago when a friend died, it was said that she died from humiliation because her daughter was pregnant. I did not believe that. After all, how could anyone take on someone else's actions as their own? Then I found myself in a similar place of taking on another's issues. Moreover, it weighed me down until I realized that it was never mine. I did not know how to control it, and I realized that I did not have to control it. I did not know but I knew who did. It was then that I felt the burden of control sliding off. Can you see how we can get bogged down with what was never ours? There comes a time that we have to let it go, and accept that we just do not know.

'I don't know' is a great place to be, for then God can mold you into what He wants. It is a grand place to be, but it is also a very interesting spot. You see, even those who profess to understand what you are going through may have only inklings of God's wonders for their life and slivers of His wonders for your life. They may attempt to offer suggestions of relief for you that may be more damaging than helpful. Look at Job's friends. I think that it is better sometimes to just sit alongside. My former pastor, the late F.G. Sampson, (Doc, we lovingly called him), used to tell his preachers, "Presence is ministry." As I grew in ministry, I understood that so very well.

Terry and I were conversing and . . . well just the whole idea that I have someone to share with helps greatly. Many ministers feel they cannot talk to someone who is not on (what they believe to be) the same level. However, you see, no one knows where God has placed those who are available. We can learn from anyone who walks close with God. Titles do not matter with God. My sister is a minister who has walked somewhat unidentified by man yet chosen by God. How do you want your life to read? Acclaimed by mankind or cherished by God? Unfortunately, what wins acclaim with people has nothing to do with what touches God's heart.

'I don't know' is a place of humility, a place of total surrender to God. It is a place of accepting that God is indeed bigger than anything we can present, even ourselves. It is a place of yielding to God. Yielding is hard. You had better believe it. Watch what happens to the seashells on the shore. They are washed up onto the sand and then back out into the water. At some point, they are crushed and become part of the sand. That is like our yielding. We let go to allow God to move us in and out, back and forth, crushing the negative parts, positioning us for what we shall become; as we become less of what we once were, and more of that in which God can work—yielded. You can say what you want, and you can handle it like you want but yielding is so hard, even more so to such a loving and giving God. We are so accustomed to doing it for ourselves. In this place, we search God out. We turn to find His will for our lives. In this place, stress can be released because we no longer need to figure our way through the fog. We just follow His voice, His aroma, His scent. Then, we move with no worries, into a place of accepting that "I don't know."

Chapter 7

My Orchid

For four years, I have had an orchid plant that was in bloom when I bought it. I watered it and cared for it but it had not bloomed again until four years later. For four years, the leaves were a promise that something may happen, and now the promise has manifested in an orchid. That was a message for me. God's promises will manifest and they will assist in my growth into what I am to be, according to His will for my life. I am still growing; I am still developing into what God has purposed for me.

There is something positive about being in fellowship and praying with sisters in ministry, sisters who love the Lord. Others may recognize that you are in a desert place and may acknowledge the fact. Those who have had their own desert place experience understand, can empathize, and may sympathize with you. The desert place is a spiritual growing experience. It is a lonely thing when God repots you, pulling you out of what is familiar, and planting you in unfamiliar ground. Real sisters will pray with you, they will come and sit with you in the aloneness of the desert place. They will not judge you; they will not give you advice, but will be there with you. You know, "Presence is Ministry." You may experience a surreal type of joy as God prunes you for what you could not handle in your former state. Real sisters will rejoice with you for the moment that you will be on the other side of the desert.

This has been a process for me. When I finally understood that it was God who chose the time for my desert travail, I stopped crying and started listening. I had to stop struggling, stop squirming, and stop trying to find my way out, stop trying to negotiate my way out. I was where I was supposed to be in this season. Did it hurt? Yes! Ask the plant that is being pruned or being repotted if, it hurts. Yes! But it is for a better good. The plant does not know that it is for the better until it blooms fully in the new pot.

Thomas Merton encourages us to "Pray for our own discovery." The orchid had a longer period between blooming than I would have imagined, but bloom it did. We have periods of blooming that we cannot determine. Merton says:

There exists some point at which I can meet God in a real and experimental contact with His infinite actuality. This is the "place" of God, His sanctuary—it is the point where my contingent being depends upon His love. Within myself is a metaphorical apex of existence at which I am held in being by my Creator. God utters me like a word containing a partial thought of Himself. A word will never be able to comprehend the voice that utters it. But if I am true to the concept that God utters in me, if I am true to the thought of Him I was meant to embody, I shall be full of His actuality and find Him everywhere in myself, and find myself nowhere. I shall be lost in Him: that is, I shall find myself. I shall be "saved . . . . To be 'saved' is to return to one's inviolate and eternal reality and to live with God." (Merton 1961, 37)

Blooming happens when you become 'saved.' I have stopped trying to analyze it all. I have stopped trying to guess what was next, or where I would be, or what would happen. I just had to stop! It was then that I began walking by faith, not by sight. It took all of that for me to understand that what I had been doing was not 'it' at all. You see, relying on God is not relying on your money, your academics, your achievements, your brain, or your acquaintances. It is doing just one thing —relying on God. God moves us to different levels in the repotting process, which allows us to bloom. I wanted to stay in Detroit to be closer to my son Marq, and my grandsons, Adonis, Trey, and Adam. It appears that God had a different plan for me. Now I am clear that wherever God sends me, I will go. He will allow me the way back to my family when I need to get to them, and He will handle their way to me when they need to get to me.

The challenge for us all is to wait during those times when it appears that nothing is happening. Can you wait when it appears that others are growing and going and you are stagnant? Can you wait? Can you wait on the promise? Wait, not on what you see, but on what you believe. Wait in peace. Oh yes, it is a challenge. Are you up to it? If you can, you will be remarkably pleased . . . if you can wait. If you can wait, you will bloom.

Chapter 8

The Proving Ground

This is a spiritual war. There are only two sides—God and Satan. An important part of the fight is to understand who you are and what belongs to you. I have gone through some grave financial times. This has caused me to attempt to find income. (Or so I thought). For every résumé I sent, for every application I completed, and with every rejection I received, I began to feel weighted down with a spirit of defeat. A well-meaning friend said that maybe I set my sights too high. At one point, I began to think she was right. Although she was 'well-meaning,' she could not possibly know God's plans for me. I held to, *"Nothing is impossible with God"* (Luke 1:37). I began to understand that this friend did not know me or understand my role in the family of Believers. For no other reason, that conversation helped me to see clearer how people can write you off. It also reminded me of something that Doc told me long ago, "You can't share your visions with valley view people." I have learned that you really cannot share your dreams or hopes with everyone. It really does not matter how close people may be to you, they do not know the conversations between you and God. Our parents taught us that not everyone is your friend. You only have a few real friends in your life, oh but there is One—Jesus.

Every time I shared my trials with someone, I lost. I lost because they did not want to hear it. Why should they? I told Terry that I had no one to lean on, to depend on . . . and she finished my sentence . . . "But Jesus, and that is where He wants you, totally yielded to Him." I told her that I was just hanging on; but at that moment in our conversation Holy Spirit said, "Let Go." I did. Now that does not mean that you should let go. That was my instruction. There are times that you fight, times that you walk away, times that you hold on, and times that you let go. When I did let go, I saw myself floating into God's arms. I realized then that many times we think we are holding on to God, when we are actually holding on to everything but God.

An hour later, I received a call from a friend that was to take me to my school three hours away in Ashland, Ohio, for a meeting. I was afraid to drive my Benz SUV, as I had not had it winterized; yet I had already received a nudging from Holy Spirit that I could drive. The friend had gotten the dates confused and could not take me. Again, I heard the Lord, "You can depend on Me. Drive the car." So, I drove down to Ashland, saw my students, handled everything I had to do, checked into a hotel, got up the next morning, and came home.

Back at home after the trip, as I went to get pizza for my grandsons, my SUV began making a roaring sound. I got the pizza (about two blocks away) and came back home, praying that it would make it, as it was getting hard to steer and making a mooing sound. I surmised that I needed power steering fluid.

The next day I called the same friend to show me where the power steering fluid went in my SUV. He said if I needed power steering fluid, then I had a leak. I looked earlier, I had no leak. Sure enough, this time, it was leaking bad, and had to be towed. My warranty provisions had it towed but it was not warranty work, and another friend called and said, "Get the work done." When the mechanic was finished, he asked me about the warning light that was on in the car. I told him the dealer said it was just a sensor and would not strand me. After he checked it, he said that the dealer should go back to school, because I had no brake lights.

Now, do with this what you want, but I had been kept from having an accident and from police tickets for two months. The SUV did not cause me trouble that could have left me stranded, I was able to go out of town and get home safely. We can depend on God. I believe that we haphazardly decide the conditions that call for dependence upon God. It is not a partial dependence, nor a haphazard dependence that He requires; but total reliance.

We look to others for our help. We fight others for what we believe is ours. Can you see the error? We look to them; we fight them. When we are clear of whom we follow, we can become clear about the fight. This is a spiritual battle, and our enemy is not flesh and blood:

For though we live in the world, we do not wage war as the world does. The weapons we fight with are not the weapons of the world. On the contrary, they have divine power to demolish stronghold. We demolish arguments and every pretension that sets itself up against the knowledge of God, and we take captive every thought to make it obedient to Christ (2 Corinthians 10:3-7).

There is a war going on and if we are not careful, we can get confused and fight the wrong thing, or not even fight at all. Our power for this war is fueled by our humility and praise. We can focus too much on the enemy and—again—lose our way. We have been given power and authority, yet our responsibility to receive guidance from Holy Spirit is tantamount on this journey.

Chapter 9

Where Is the Love?

I am waiting on and watching what God is doing in my life. It took me a while to get to this place. I have not had money to pay bills, yet I no longer panic about them. Too many times, we say we are waiting and watching, but are we really waiting? Are we really watching? I know that God is working through me and with me. It does not feel good, but it feels safe. That in itself is major. How many times do you just need to feel safe? There is a line in the movie, *"The Holiday,"* when the thirty something love torn heroine, Iris, receives a corsage from ninety-year old legendary screenwriter, Arthur. He says, "I guess it's corny to give a corsage." She answers, "I'm looking for corny." Along the same line, people need to feel safe. They are looking for that safety, that "loving one another" that we are to do as believers. In addition, you cannot tell them to run to God, to try God, without following that advice yourself. Others need to see your witness, and that witness is missing today. Many believers are afraid to share their testimony; yet there is always someone that can benefit from your witness. You must be clear when the time is right for you to share. Holy Spirit will guide you; you follow that guidance. Holy Spirit actually places you in position to witness to another.

Someone needs to see where you have fallen, where you have been hurt, have suffered, and how you are surviving. Holy Spirit gave me that simple message a few weeks ago. I thought I would tell this story when I had made it though this leg of my journey, but Holy Spirit said, "Tell it now."

This desert place is a proving ground for me, no doubt about it; yet it is more than just about me. None of us goes through what we go through for ourselves alone. The proving ground is a major examination on what I have retained as a child of God, as a servant of God. It is facing what frightens me the most. It is facing myself and seeing just how I measure up to what God has for me. I don't! I do not measure up, but I'm trying to do better. I do not deserve this opportunity, but God loves me that much. When my final exam comes, I pray to be ready. God is teaching me, and loving me through this time; yet others will benefit. It is their way out of and into safe arms. Do I really like being the bait, the guinea pig? No, but it is humbling to understand that God knows me well enough that to trust me in this. Have you seen My servant Job? Have you seen My servant Emily? That is who I am, Yahweh's servant. Do not mistake that sentiment; I am not the only servant, not me alone. Anyone who claims to have accepted this call into divine ministry is a servant.

Sounds simple? No, it is difficult, and challenging, and frightening; but it is doable. There have been times when I have cried out, "Is this really You?" "Is this what You had in mind?" "What am I doing wrong?" "Why can't I be still?" That was something my mother used to say to me when I was little. I was into everything; and she would ask, "Can't you be still?" Before this season, I found myself running to catch up, to get out there, to be in the know. In this place, I had to let go, to get still. Well actually, it takes three things for me: Let go of my will, yield to God, and accept God's will for my life. I cannot handle this alone, I have parts of me that are still untrusting, still unyielding, still afraid to let go. My heart understands, but my head flounders. It has to be that, why else would I not trust the One who has kept me to this point? In spite of all this, He gives me sprinkles of His love, sprinkles of His grace, and sprinkles of His provision. That really is more than enough. All we need is a sprinkle; all we can handle is a sprinkle, little streams of God's love. Then there are showers of God's love. My, My! To be in the showers of God's love! To be in that place where God's anointing flows. Another professor, colleague, and dear friend, Terry Wardle, says, "To be under the spout where the glory comes out." We can, but we have to accept the sprinkles before we can handle the showers.

"All authority in heaven and on earth has been given to Me. Therefore go and make disciples of all nations, baptizing them in the name of the Father and of the son and of the Holy spirit and teaching them to obey everything I have commanded you. And surely I am with you always, to the very end of the age" (Matthew 28:18, 19). In contemplating that great commission and what it means to me I had a new revelation. I know that Jesus is with me, but why do I doubt? Oh yeah, I say I doubt myself, but let's be real, I doubt God. Unfortunately, I am not alone. *"When they saw Him, they worshiped Him-but some of them still doubted"* (Matthew 28:17 NLT). Have you noticed that sometimes 'buts' will mess you up? The passage says, "but some of them still doubted." The

ones being referred to are the disciples, those close to Jesus, not the everyday people in the crowd. These were the core disciples who had walked with Jesus, they had witnessed the marvels of His ministry, but they still doubted. That passage spoke to me, because I waver. I still have tiny doubts that God can keep me through all. There I said it. Run and tell that. Oh—you can't—He already knows. I still doubt, and when I do I miss out on the peace God affords. You see, I know God has kept me through this strange time, and I know there is much to be learned here, and I know that I am to be still. So, why do I doubt? Why can't I rid myself of this human nature that wants to handle it all myself? This nature that wants to take of myself, and I know that I cannot do it alone. It is about me not accepting God's love in its entirety. God loves me more than anyone walking has or can ever will. When I rest in that, I can feel His love, and I can breathe, I can live, I can share His love.

We used to sing this song at my home church in Nashville, "Too many people doubt Him, but I can't live without Him." Long ago, I could relate only to the latter, but now I can relate to the former. Help my unbelief! It is a struggle. However, I must let go. What about you? Where are you in the Matthew passage? Are you worshiping, yet doubting? Can you really worship and doubt? No, you cannot; that is division right there. You cannot effectively worship and doubt. I believe that you can praise with a tad of doubt, and in your sincere praise, doubt will diminish. From there you can enter into worship. Find out about yourself. Take a look at what you believe. Try to get a better understanding of who you are and where you are in this. And even then, find peace in your knowledge and growth. You cannot do this alone. There is something positive about having a spiritual director to aid you in your growth.

You seek love from people, you crave attention, you run after everything. You want to feel loved, so you demand it from others. You do for others hoping they will reciprocate. You misuse your love and shame others into loving you through their guilt. After all, why shouldn't they want to give back? Ah, but God! God patiently waits for you, loving you unconditionally. That is some powerful stuff! I asked one of my students and a friend, Teresa, for a song for my play, "End, The Beginning." After reading the script and working with "New Creation," my liturgical dancers, Teresa sang acappella in the play while "New Creation," performed. Her song is entitled, "He's Waiting for His People to Love Him." I don't think she ever put the song to music. I don't think she should. I do hope she records it, and if she does, you really should get it. When you hear her sing it with her rich alto voice, you can feel the pain of unrequited love. To hear the notes flow from God through Teresa tugging your heart to love God back is a precious moment in time. The love relationship with Jesus is so precious that it pulls you into a place in time, suspended as He waits for you to love Him back. God waits for you with love, grace, joy, peace, freedom, comfort. Because God has already loved you, you can love God back.

"I trust You Lord." It really does not matter how many times we say it. Unless it is from our heart, it does not work. "I trust You

Lord." Take a piece of paper. Answer that question; you should face where you really are. How do you measure up? Where do you place your trust?

Let us pray that your eyes are opened to the all-encompassing love of God, your heart be surrendered to the guidance of Holy Spirit, and your path be true to the walk of Jesus. That is spiritual transformation.

Chapter 10

Broken Blessing

My, my, look at how God works. It has been eight years since the Lord told me that I would live on ministry and my writing. I have retired and had a great time finishing two degrees. I can see glimpses of my writing as being lucrative, but I am not there yet.

In his book, *Full Service: Moving from Self-Serve Christianity to Total Servanthood*, Siang-Yang Tan says:

> It is only when our expectations are frustrated, our plans are thwarted, our dream shattered, and our desires withered into nothingness that we know firsthand the powerlessness and poverty of a child, and hence experience and rest in the love of God for us! In the brokenness of true servanthood, deep rest in the Lord can be experienced. There is servanthood and rest. (Tan 2006, 105)

Reading that piece brought me back to what I was doing at this point in my life. I am a broken person; Henri Nouwen calls it, "Wounded Healer." I shall call it, 'Broken Blessing.' I have been broken, and I have been blessed. Blessing is not that you are always getting something from God, but that you are being guided by and provided for by Holy Spirit. It does not mean that you are being showered with money or fame or name or . . . well you get it. There is a blessing in the brokenness; of course, it is not easy, it is never fun, but it is a part of the journey. Therefore, as a 'broken blessing,' I hold on and wait for my next direction.

Can you see Jesus at His last supper with His disciples? He took the bread. It is a wonderful thing to be "taken," to be "claimed," by Jesus. When He takes us, His mark is on us. Taking us removes us from being claimed by the world. It is clearly an experience as we are His and He is ours, and that is quite unlike what you experience in any relationship. We are His servants, His vessels to be used. As His own, Jesus pours Himself into us and shapes us for how we are to be used. We are no longer our own. It does not mean that we cannot think for ourselves. On the contrary, we make decisions based not only on what we know or about what we see, but also on whose we are.

In our family, our parents admonished my sister and me to act like a "Morton." There were some things that we just did not do; and there were traits that we had, as a "Morton." One such trait was a strong work ethic and a sense of self. We watched both parents work hard many times, with two jobs each to provide for our family. We learned our heritage as "Yates," maternal, and "Morton," paternal. As a child of God there is a way that you should act that reflects the love of God, it can be done because of our being made in God's image. You learn in the body of Christ what the community of believers means to the body.

When God 'takes us' we are removed from the world, and that is a major thing right there. We are in the world yet we are protected by God's amazing care. We see, we live, yet we can be at peace with our condition. Paul says, *"Whatever state I find myself, to be content"* (Philippians 1:11). We can be content leaning on and learning from Holy Spirit. Being taken by Jesus is clearly a moment . . . as we are His and His alone. We are His servants; we are His vessels; and He pours Himself into us to be used for His glory. We are molded into what He has decided for our destiny. Yes, it really should be a great thing, but yes, it really is a hard thing. When Jesus claims you as His own to be used, you begin a journey that moves you away from situations where you are comfortable. You are grown through unknown places and moved around obstacles. The growth disturbs your spirit yet brings a peace as you are undone and redone by God. I think that is why so many people who go to church are so afraid of what may happen to them. Sometimes they are unnerved about what is happening to them under the power of Holy Spirit. Playing church cannot prepare you for your destiny. Being church should aid you through discipleship in discerning the voice and will of God. Unfortunately, too many churches are playing too many games with God's will for the church. As a result, people are being lost.

That term, 'To be taken,' is a paradox. It is wonderful, yet scary; protected, yet pierced. Do you get the picture? Okay, through it all, it really is what you want. It is better than anything society has to offer. It is your own "get out of jail free" card. Those in the church, even those who profess to be claimed by God, have attempted to tear me down. I have watched their tactics and often wondered, "Why did they waste their time?" You see, for everything they tried against me, God allowed me to use it as another step up along my journey. I suppose that one could call it a part of human nature, but that is what we are to kill—that humanness. We are to die daily to self. It is no picnic, but it is a grand peace knowing that God is indeed working both with you and on your behalf. As Jesus took the bread, He claims us from the clutches of the world, and brings us into another level in Him. Just the thought of being claimed by Jesus should provide some comfort knowing that, as they used to sing when I was small, "He's working it out for my good." A gathering of believers who have been claimed by Jesus should be a place of excitement, of power, of manifestation. Even with a pruning, those pruned should be ready to offer encouragement: *"Therefore, since we are surrounded by such a great cloud of witnesses, let us throw off everything that hinders and the sin that so easily entangles, and let us run with perseverance the race marked out before us"* (Hebrews 12:1). That should be what the church does as a body of believers. Just think—we have been claimed by Jesus. That is something very wonderful, but there is more.

After Jesus took the bread, He blessed it. Just the thought of being claimed by Jesus should be quite a blessing yet it goes farther. Can we even fathom what being blessed by God means? Can we begin to understand the depth of that blessing? Can a peach know when the sun has kissed it so tenderly that it ripens? Can night understand just what it is to succumb to day? Can you imagine what being blessed by God means? Most of the time, our idea of blessed by God is so in error. God's blessing may not mean that good things always happen. It means that He is with us in the moment, the situation, and the event and because of that, we indeed can hold on. It means that we are totally in God's care: *"My prayer is not for them alone. I pray also for those who will believe in me through their message, that all of them may be one, Father, just as you are in me and I am in you"* (John 17:20, 21). Just to know that you belong to one who so lovingly cares for you in spite of yourself is blessing enough.

Paul blesses the church at Ephesus, *"May you have the power to understand, as all God's people should, how wide, how long how high, and how deep His love really is. May you experience the love of Christ; though it is so great you will never fully understand it. Then you will be filled with the fullness of life and power that comes from God"* (Ephesians 3:16-19 NLT). Paul's blessing is my blessing for you along your journey.

'After Jesus blessed it, then He broke the bread.' I heard it preached long ago that Jesus takes you and blesses you then breaks you in order to use you, just as He did the bread. This breaking is not a punishment but a process of refining. He breaks us to get the best out of us. Oh yeah, it hurts; which I could do without; and the process of taking, blessing, and breaking does not happen just once but over and over again. The breaking gets a little more intense with our being refined to the best that we can be for the mission He has for us. So while I could do without the hurt, I want the process so I can be perfected for God's use.

I am at a breaking place and it has been like nothing I have experienced before. After the hurt, the humiliation of not having a way to care for myself, after the frightening feeling of not knowing what will happen, after all these years taking care of myself, now, not knowing what to do; then watching, and working through the feelings of my hurt because my church leadership wanted nothing to do with me. After watching a shepherd leave the sheep scattered, what do you do then? Well I cried, I had a two-month pity party—me, myself, and I. No one else would come. Believe me, we three were the wrong ones to invite. I had left God off the invitation and that was the wrong thing. Out of everything, I thought I knew, I found out that I had no clue about so many things. It is in this breaking place that I have begun to breathe. It is at this financial lowest place in my life that I had no plan B. I just did not know what to do. But at this place, I had an ah-ha moment: With Jesus, you don't need a plan B! With Jesus as plan A, nothing else is needed but to get clear directions from Holy Spirit.

If you are in the place where everything is going well, and everything is doing fine, hold on, your breaking is coming. It can come in so many ways, but I promise you it is for your best. It is a part of that 'all things plan' of God. You know, *"And we know that in all things God works for the good of those who love Him, who have been called according to His purpose"* (Romans 8:28). The breaking is so that God can get more of you from you. More of who you really are instead of what others and even you are trying to make you to be. Even now, I ask God, "What are you doing?" I can ask that because of our relationship. And I can ask,

"Which way shall I go?" The comforting thing is that I do not know what it all means but I know that it is a part of God's 'all things' plan for my life.

This is a journey and the exciting thing about the journey is that it is not ours to map out, but it is ours to follow what has been mapped out for us. God has blessed me, broken me, and uses me for His glory. Come on, I would rather not have to be broken, but it is a part of growth. The break is necessary. I ponder how we can get so entrenched in difficult times and lose focus. Even now, I see this period as a pressing to get the best out of me, like a winepress to grapes, or an olive press to olives. In turn, I am to press into this time and yes, find God there.

In one vision, I saw me fighting off an extremely large wolf with only a staff. I was fighting to keep the sheep behind me safe. I did not quite understand it, but the Lord said that I needed to know how to fight *this* kind of wolf. Now so many things came to my mind when I saw this. The first one was that the wolf was a person that was causing havoc in my life at that time. I soon understood that it was not a person, but situations that I needed be aware of in order to be equipped to maneuver them. God does not call His children anything but what they are, His children. People are people; they are not demons; although some can act like it at times. They can be influenced by demonic forces. Actually, you can if you are not careful; thus the need for prayer and obedience. That is a good reminder. Whenever we feel we need to talk about someone or call that person out of his or her purpose, we have just abused our purpose.

Marq said something to me recently about his sons, whom he calls "Mini me's." My middle grandson, Trey, has been pinching the baby, Adam; and Marq has warned him about that. As Marq was sharing the last incident he said that both of them came from him and he loved them equally; if one of them hurts the other, it hurts him. Then he made the relation to us and God. Since we come from God, when we hurt one another, it hurts God. Wow! Can you see the revealing of Jesus command? *"Love one another. As I have loved you, so you must love one another. By this all men will know that you are my disciples, if you love one another"* (John 13: 24).

Now back to my vision. God used the imagery of a wolf in my vision. I pulled some three Scriptures: *"Watch out for false prophets. They come to you in sheep's clothing but inwardly they are ferocious wolves"* (Matthew 7:15). *"I am sending you out like sheep among wolves. Therefore be as shrewd as snakes and innocent as doves"* (Matthew 10:16). *"I am sending you out like lambs among wolves"* (Luke 10:3).

It is interesting that Jesus uses the imagery of wolves. To get a better understanding of wolves and their hunting style, I will use something Frederick Sampson III shared at convocation a few years ago about the hunting style of wolves (Sampson, 2003):

Wolves hunt in packs, they don't hunt alone. When they attack they look for the prey, pick out their prey, those who are weak, lost, old, or wounded. Then the wolves run the herd until the young and weak can't keep up and the old can no longer move. They isolate their prey, surrounding them and taunting them by biting at the prey. The wolves don't kill the prey yet, but just toy with them. Bear in mind, when you are in a circle and you are bit in the front you move back, if you are bit on the side, you move to the other side. In the circle, wherever you move you move into another bite. You jump from one mouth into another. (Can you see it?) And then from every angle, the wolves bite at the ankles until their prey, crippled, fall to their knees. Yet the wolves still don't kill. They move in and begin to eat the prey alive. And the victim gives up and decides to die. That is what the enemy does.

We can help ourselves by staying out of the mouth of the wolves when we understand how wolves hunt, for the enemy does the same thing. Demons are ravenous wolves seeking whom they can devour. In that vision, I had to protect the spiritually weak, the babes in Christ, and those who were wandering. I had to keep them safe from the wolf. I had to know how to fight.

A few days following the vision of the wolf, I had a dream that brought quite a few things into perspective for me. There was a cabin of sorts with quite a few young people sitting at the foot of the cabin bunk beds laughing and talking. It was a large room and I had gathered them there for an informal meeting. We had just finished the meeting when a large snake entered the cabin and slowly crossed around the beds. I whispered to the young people to get still and not move. Before I could think of what to do a much larger snake crept into the cabin and began wrestling with the other snake. These two were entangled and then the larger one swallowed the first one and began slinking around the room. It moved slowly and methodically over beds and around the feet of the young people. All I could do was say, "Don't move; be still." I did not know what to do!

Just then, an angel appeared and she had on a blue dress (now we know that they have no gender). She left a small wire cage on the floor. While I was wondering why she didn't stay and what was I going to do, that large snake slinked all of its long body right into that little wire cage. As soon as its tail was in, I slammed the cage door shut. Nervously, I then lifted the cage, which was as light as a feather, took it outside and threw it off a cliff into the water, near the cabin.

I awakened from that dream resolved to "be still," as God does have everything under control in my life. There are so many situations that we find ourselves in; and we try to make sense of them. When we get still we have the opportunity to know that He is God (Psalm 46:10b); it places us in the blessed position to move. This journey is not about others and how they affect us, it is about how we react in our relationship in God; and that determines how we handle others. That is so difficult to do, but it can be done. It is a difficult walk, and at times— a struggle, yet it is all part of our journey. As I pondered that dream, I remembered that the young people trusted and obeyed me. That is a feat in itself! It is indeed a grand responsibility we have in caring for others.

Chapter 11

Every Round

As a "broken blessing," I have learned when to stand still and when to walk away. I have learned that I do not need to explain my actions to others that are not on the same leg of the journey. There comes a time when we recognize that while many are on this journey, quite a few may not be where we are, and we may not be where others are. Wherever we find ourselves on this journey there is much we can learn from one another.

In Paul's letters to the church at Ephesus, God gave these gifts to the church: apostles, prophets, evangelists, pastors, and teachers. Their responsibility is to equip God's people to do the work of the church, and build up the body of Christ, until we come to such unity in our faith and knowledge of God's Son that we will be mature and full grown in the Lord, measuring up to the full stature of Christ (Ephesians 4:11-14 NLT). Mature and full-grown—what does that look like? It appears to me that really is a very tall order. How can we become mature in Christ? What does maturity in full grown in Christ look like? How do we measure up to the full stature of Christ? With all of the stuff in our way, with all the junk we have to deal with, with the junk we make ourselves. How do we measure up? It is a great thing that

God sees more in us than we can see in ourselves. Look at Jesus' character as presented in the New Testament. Define Jesus, and what you will find is what we can look like. After all, Jesus came to show us how to walk like Him, act like Him, and grow in maturity in Him. We have the ability to become spiritually transformed because we are made in God's image (Genesis 1:16). So it really is possible.

I speak of Divine Favor with more spiritual maturity now. God's favor is more than when all things are working right. God's favor keeps you when nothing appears to be going right around you. A few years ago in the movie *"Men in Black,"* the two heroes, agents J and K, played by Will Smith and Tommie Lee Jones, had just shot down an escaping space ship manned by aliens. As it came crashing to the earth skidding toward them, K stood firm without flinching. J began to worry and kept glancing at K for assurance. The ship stopped right before them. Nothing was going to happen to them that day. Can you see it? You can have that quiet peace in the midst of a surging storm. It is like watching a tsunami coming your way and you are resting assured of Jesus' provincial care, so you stand. You can rest assured in His provincial care. Then things not only happen to you, they happen around you, they come upon you, you know, like the blessings. Each round, each leg of the journey, should be a transforming one.

Chapter 12

Ravens

Have you ever considered ravens as hope? Yes, we know Edgar Allen Poe's famous poem, "The Raven," yet we find ravens are mentioned at least one time in Scripture, in the seventeenth chapter of 1 Kings where the prophet Elijah was fed by ravens: *"The ravens brought him bread and meat in the morning and bread and meat in the evening, and he drank from the brook"* (1 Kings 17:6). So that is what you know, but let me tell you about my ravens. Now of course, I would have wanted to handle things myself, but it was not what God has had for me. After all my crying and all my moaning, I had to stop and watch the ravens. A mentor told me that God was sending ravens to keep me, and she was so right.

My porch steps had separated from the front porch and I was concerned because winter was coming, and someone could get hurt on the steps, especially when it snowed. Estimates for the repair ranged from one thousand leading all the way to three thousand dollars. The quotes were well out of my reach, money was nowhere to be found. I was waiting on a check and it was not that much. Then the postal carrier held my mail for two weeks because of the dangerous step. Can you see the irony?

A few weeks earlier, someone had left his number on a sheet of paper in my mailbox about repairing the steps. I did not call him because I did not know if I could trust his work. Now my back was against the wall, so I took a chance and called him. There is something about not receiving your mail when you are waiting on a check that will cause you to rethink your position. The guy that left the note was a preacher and he asked when I wanted the work done. I told him it depended on the cost. He came out that Sunday evening, looked at the porch, and gave me a price of one hundred fifty dollars. I couldn't believe it! My son and family had arrived for dinner and games. The guy said he would take about an hour. Two hours later, he was done. We were finished eating and were playing games. The porch looked great. The preacher blessed me with an affirmation from God. He said he would have normally charged two hundred fifty to three hundred fifty dollars, but the Lord gave him the figure to charge me. All I had was two hundred dollars. Can you see the blessing? Ravens.

A few months later, a water pipe rotted in my kitchen in the dead of winter and I had no way to get it fixed. I heard repair estimates from one thousand dollars up to three thousand dollars; that was way out of my financial reach. Something had to happen; I did not know what or how. The water was seeping under my stone tile floors. A friend told her husband, a brother minister, about my plight. He called and gave me a number to call and the repair guy came out in about a half hour, which was a feat for such a cold snowy day. As the repair guy was giving me the estimate, the doorbell rang with the brother minister at the door. He walked in right as the estimate was being quoted. He heard the figure, wrote the check for the repair guy, and left. Look at God! It just brings to mind how Jesus paid the price for our life with His life. Jesus wrote the check ahead of time for us with His life. It does not matter how disconnected we are from God; Jesus paid the price for us to be reconnected. Jesus does not hold it over our heads what He has done for us. No, we have free will. I think we miss that sometimes.

These are just two of the monetary issues. I have had 'ravens' to call me to come and pick up groceries they had bought me, or they delivered groceries to me, or they told me to check my mailbox for money they left for me. However, there has been so much more during this period. I have come to understand that it has never been about the money, but about my faith in God's provision. One morning, as I was making the bed God sat me down and said, "You trust me here, but not here; here but not here." I understood so well. Why do we not allow God control of all aspects of our life? It was never about the loss of money for me, it was about the lack of complete trust in God. Sometimes you have to go through, and you can, if you allow God the chance to lead. There will be times that God will send the ravens. A close friend, herself a raven for many people, says that ravens have small beaks. We must trust that God will send enough ravens and that the ravens can make enough trips.

In that Kings passage, Elijah was fed by the ravens. In my life, I have been fed by the ravens. Has God allowed the ravens to feed you? It can come in so many ways, but it does come. God has a way of allowing a blessing to be blessed. It is so cool. You never know how it will come, and you must be faithful to be a blessing to another. It is indeed the least costly, safest investment you can make; the returns are too great to count. The song we used to sing when we were small speaks volumes here, "You can't beat God's giving, no matter how you try." Watch for the ravens.

Chapter 13

Connect the Dots

Have you ever played the game of "connect the dots?" Surely, you must have when you were small. You are faced with a page of dots that seemingly appear to have some kind of meaning, some kind of pattern but you are not sure what it is. You do know that you cannot just start anywhere and get where you think you want to go. So how do you get there? You start at the dot numbered '1' or lettered 'A,' and follow the numbers or letters as high as you can count. Along the way, you begin to see the picture. There are times you may think that you have a clue, you think that you can see where the dots are going, but then the picture takes on a different shape. You find the final picture was not what you thought it would have been. Okay, so now you have connected the dots.

The Lord showed me "connect the dots." I was trying to stay focused on how to keep everything up and spinning, yet failing miserably. God told me, "Look back." He showed me that He had been the one guiding me through my maze of dots. I looked back and as He pointed out major moves in my life. He told me to look around where I was now (or where I thought I was). He explained that He guides me through the dots and only when I see Him face to face will I understand the big picture. My, my! There is no way that we can understand the picture that has been drawn for us; but we can follow the dots. It is all a part of the journey.

I have had a few rough lessons. I believe we all go through our rough times for a reason. I do not want you to go through lessons as mine, especially when there is a so much more peaceful way. I went for a year and a half with minimal income, yet the major bills were paid, the house, car, and insurance. Remember my ravens? Yet I prayed for a way to make income so I could function for myself (Miss self-reliant). I launched a very "lucrative" career (or so they said it would be), yet I was worse off financially than I was when I had little income. And the message? It is not about relying on self. It is not about the position. It is about allowing God to place me where I am going. It is not about the money. Don't get me wrong, yes, we need money to live; it allows us to manage part of our core needs.

I watched "20 Greatest Gospels" on the country music station on cable. Many of the songs took me back to my roots when even Blacks would listen to the country station in Tennessee because that is where they could hear gospel. We still have so much to learn from one another and from God, if only we would listen. As I listened, it brought memories. Many of the country songs were about when we see Jesus' face and looking for His return. I thought how much they were like gospel songs in the Bahamas. These songs offer hope for those who need hope while looking to the return of Jesus. I thought how so many songs in the church today offer no hope, but hype with a beat. Of course, the message will reach whom it will reach; the gospel must still be shared.

That is how those dots get connected. It does not matter how we share as long as we are witnesses of that Divine Love through our actions.

I talked to a prayer partner about her daughter who had been in the hospital. She had realized that the ordeal suffered by her daughter and her hospitalization was not about her or her daughter alone. As we chatted, I understood just that; the Lord had shown me a few weeks prior that what I was experiencing was not for me alone. Now, there it was again; those dots were being connected. Previously, within a two-week period, four preachers called to talk with me. All of them confirmed what the Lord had shown me. So now, again I was hearing a prayer partner confirming, "It is not about me." It is not about us. It is not about you. It is never about us alone. Although we go through what we go through, we do not go through it alone. Our experiences are not for us alone. Yes, it feels like we go through it alone, but there is always someone else is going through. That is where we can help one another. That is where our testimony comes into play. That is where we can help one another, hold to one another. If we are to get a better grasp of loving one another, then we must understand that we are not alone. Others are affected by what happens to us, and we are affected by what happens to others. You know, it is the African spirit of Mbutu, "I am because we are." We are all in this together.

While I was a union steward in Tennessee, I had tee shirts made to help increase our sense of unity as union workers. You may have seen the image yourself. It is of a snow-covered house surrounded by snow everywhere, and yet the flakes were still falling. The scene now reminds me so much of Detroit. Anyway, the caption reads, "A snowflake is a fragile thing, but look what they can do when they stick together." As believers, we may believe we cannot accomplish much; but in community, with other believers, look at what we can accomplish. Look at the prayer power!

Lack of finances has always been a hindrance to me. I have always wanted to be able to do what I want but I never cared about being rich. Now I can say, "I have had some, now I don't have." I recognize that too much worry about my future placed a wedge between God and me. Jesus clearly encourages us, *"Therefore do not worry about tomorrow, for tomorrow will worry about itself"* (Matthew 6:34). That in itself was liberating. Now I can see, I can hear, I can feel, I can watch God's movement in my life! You see, I worried because others felt I should worry; but others are not on the same path, their dots are not arranged the same. Therefore, they cannot possibly understand which way you should go. In order to follow your dots you determine what has wedged between you and God. Find out how your attention has been diverted, and surrender that. You can surrender it or He will help you do it. He loves you that much.

Chapter 14

Living in Grace

As I showered, I fretted that I desperately needed to send out two payments for life insurance. Then I realized that I had already paid for the next month, and I was living in the grace period. That works with life insurance because you actually pay ahead one month. As I pondered, I thought how living in the "past due" state in life has taught me more about God's love. Sometimes we cannot appreciate living in God's grace because we think we have done it all ourselves. Living in God's grace is made possible because Jesus' life, death, and resurrection paid it ahead for all forever. Hopefully I can share more about living in His grace or living with His divine favor.

It has taken all of this desert experience to get me to a place of total reliance on God. My prayer is to stay right here, in thought. If I can stay focused on that alone, I do not need to see what is ahead, because God will guide. I regret many decisions that I made while younger and even now, but I cannot linger in regrets. At times, I did not step out in faith enough in what God told me to do, and how I was to do it. No, I allowed others to interfere with what I heard, and I followed what they said. Now you know that really did not make sense. You see, they did not hear what I heard and that caused me to doubt myself on what I had heard. It also caused me to settle for less than what God had planned for me. No more!

How many times have you received instructions from God but you allowed others to interfere with your execution of those instructions? You know, someone who told you that you could not possibly be right? Think about it. There is always someone that will cause you to doubt yourself and what you have heard. Doc used to say, "You cannot share your dreams with valley view people." I have finally understood that valley view people cannot possibly understand the mountain vision you have received. If they could, they would filter it through different lens than you. We all have different filters as we all have different experiences that have brought us to this moment. How odd is that when you decide to follow another instead of Divine urgings? It can bring one out of living in grace.

Jesus warned the disciples, *"I tell you the truth, anyone who will not receive the kingdom of God like a little child will never enter it"* (Mark 10:15). I believe that is a sure way of living in grace, to become childlike in our trust of God. I think that is the beauty of childlike innocence. As a child, I trusted what Jesus said. Now, as an adult with more experience, I have trusted others more and God less. How totally backward is that? Oh, but I am on the right path now.

While I was in Florida for my nephew and niece's college graduations, I was walking along the beach at the house where we stayed. Holy Spirit told me to pull out the revelations He had given me and write them in one book. Simple enough, yet I have not done it. Father, forgive me. Again, why do we fail so often to obey God? What is that about? So now I have started to do just that.

While on the beach, I saw a small bird walking along the beach, a pelican swooping down for fish, and a shark circling in the water, all were searching for food. It was a thing of beauty to see. The shark spies out the food, circles, and kills. The pelican searches, identifies, and swoops down. The little bird waits, sees, and grabs. Each had its own way of getting food. But it is the bird that, many times, is victim to everything larger. The bird waits for the waves to roll out, then runs to pick the fish pieces that have been left ashore. He pecks around then runs back to miss the waves coming in. The bird is so small. While it can fly, it cannot scoop down into the water and grab what it sees as the pelican does. The bird must wait for the waves to deliver what it needs from the water. So it waits. The bird does not circle around as the shark and then attacks, but it waits.

I watched what was going on and I wondered about the bird, the pelican, and the shark that had now moved farther out in the water. I hear, "What do you see?" I understand there is something here that is beyond my sight. I know the fish are there. I cannot see them but they are there. Why else would the bird, the pelican, and the shark wait? "What do you see?" There is something more than this casual walk on the beach. Even as I jot this down, I hear a plane flying overhead. I hear it, but I do not see it. What can I learn from the bird, the pelican, and the shark? Ah-ha!

What does this scene have to do with anything? As Doc used to say, "Glad you asked." We are that bird that waits on the promise of provision. Just like the bird, we cannot reach into the waves for the food, but we wait on God's promise of provision. We must understand what we can handle and then wait on the promise. We can handle the wee bit that is deposited for us to enjoy. Now understand the bits are so much more than mere size. The wee bit is what we can handle. We do not have to search for it; we do not need to spy it out and maneuver to get it. While we watch and wait, we learn to steer clear of the dangers in our lives. Call it "Sea Wisdom."

Chapter 15

'Here' Is Relevant

'Here' is relevant. 'Here' is an adverb used to refer to this place or this time. It draws attention to a point or place near, as opposed to 'there.' We all get to that place of 'here' through many avenues: We come through, we come out of, and we come into, all to get 'here.' 'Here' is only relevant for now because our journey should move us closer to our destiny. We do not stay here, thus the 'here' changes.

We face many obstacles, yet our biggest obstacle is always self. Self will cause us to give up the journey and miss our destination. We are all at different places in our lives and one person cannot judge another because of the place in which they are. Even if you have been where I am now, we are not at the same place. Even if we stand side by side and experience the very same thing our experiences will be different, we will process differently, because our 'here' is not the same. One cannot know exactly what another is thinking or feeling about an event or stimulus primarily because we have been there. One can only experience that event through a personal encounter. Why did I say that? You cannot tell me what I am thinking, or how I should handle my problem solely on your experience. You can only offer presence and prayers, at best. We must be careful as ministers, as leaders, how we guide others. (That is why helping one to experience a healing touch from Holy Spirit is so important).

I saw three red birds today. At first, there were two in the yard, then three. Why is that so significant to me? The one red bird caught my attention; the two together held my attention, but the three together caused me to look beyond what I was witnessing and to praise God. I have very rarely seen two redbirds together, but to see three! I am at a pivotal place in my life, and God's creation assures me that I am not alone. When I saw the two, Holy Spirit let me know that I am not alone, when I saw the three red birds it affirmed that the Trinity held me secure. Yes, God can bring tidbits of hope any way He chooses, and He does just that. I do not want to miss any of it. He is all, over all, and with all. That is such a great comfort. The writer of Hebrews says, "... *Just as the builder of a house has greater honor than the house itself. For every house is built by someone, but God is the builder of everything*" (Hebrews 3:3b-4). It assures me that God is everywhere, even in my 'here.'

'Here' is relevant. We cannot judge others on what they should "be doing" or how they should "act." We have no clue what that means for them. We do not know their 'here' because their 'here' is not our 'here.' We can point them toward watching God's moves in their life. That is a better way to aid someone in recognizing their place of being, their 'here.' Life is a challenge, a journey that we all make and it depends on the mission. Some people choose fame, money, you know. I choose worship on the journey. At times, I do not do that very well, yet I am invited into that place of peace right here. That place of peace keeps me coming back, keeps me wanting more of what God has for me. It is not over there, but right here.

Chapter 16

The Name

I have too many bosses. I was with my middle grandson on his school trip and my cell phone rang. Earlier, I had talked to my supervisor about one of my clients. Now another supervisor from a different position calls. It was the director from an academic program of which I am involved. He was concerned that I had missed a meeting eight months prior. He had determined (in error) that I was not sincere about the program. I had been to the last meeting four months prior and began to defend my position assuring him of my commitment to the program. Our meetings are once every four months and in the four years since the program's inception, I had only missed two meetings. I finished the call disturbed at having to defend my position. Then I realized it was not about my loyalty to a program but there were underlying issues. I could not tell him at that time that I had missed the one meeting because I had to take a job and was in training. I could not be at that one meeting because I had to live; I had to pay my bills. He expected me to pledge my commitment when I had been there and others had not. At that point, I understood I could not promise anything because I do not know what will happen in the future. I concluded from the call, "I have too many bosses." Each one wants me to perform for their specialty area, and at times, they overlap. Each one offers something that bottom line, controls me, whether it is an easier way, success, monetary compensation. Yet none could offer what I needed—peace. While I knew this to be true, I still allowed them too much control.

There really can be only one who has control, one master. The Word says, *"No one can serve two masters. Either he will hate the one and love the other, or he will be devoted to the one and despise the other. You cannot serve both God and money"* (Matthew 6:24). This does not mean that we cannot have more than one stream of income; it does mean we cannot let that income dominate our total time. If we give more service to money than to God, that becomes a dangerous place from which to operate.

I have too many bosses, not because I am trying to do everything. Maybe I should be doing what God has told me, "Let go." He really is the one in charge of my life. So if I have something to do, I just do. Moreover, if it takes letting go of one thing in order to advance the Kingdom, I will, but right now, with my saved self, I have entirely too many bosses. Then I understood! We allow our lives too many connections with negative things, people, situations, and thoughts. We receive instructions from too many places, too many people. The only way we can be effective on this journey is to sort the connections through a filter of the Holy Spirit. When we allow Holy Spirit to disconnect and reconnect some things, then we can travel more confident along the journey. We follow a higher calling, which will humble us into a safe place. There is only one boss, one master, and His name is above every name—Jesus.

Chapter 17

The Rest

What happens in the Sabbath's Rest? You can bloom. To bloom is to grow and flourish. Why are you afraid to bloom? You have been invited into this place of rest, where you bloom, where you flourish with God, and you cannot refuse. When you are invited in, you can indeed rest and indeed bloom. God gave me "Sabbath's Rest," a few years ago. Some of what I have learned about Sabbath's Rest is that while it is an invitation, you cannot refuse God. Boy, how ignorant have I been! Here I am looking at one thing that He told me, but I am missing something else altogether. God is a Whole, and we do a grave injustice when we do not take account the whole of God. Grant it, we can never understand the fullness of God, but we can accept the wholeness. We cannot separate the parts of the Whole. We cannot take part of Him and then not take the rest of Him. To accept the Whole is to trust the Word fully, to seek guidance continually. Yes, I do want to enter in. Now, what does that mean? What happens when we do not accept? Well, how can you refuse God? He invites us just as He invited the Israelites many times to turn back to Him. What on earth is the struggle with that? Why is it so hard to trust Him?

There is a passage in Hebrews that I wrestled with for quite a while, *"Today, if you hear His voice, do not harden your hearts"* (Hebrews 3:7-8 & 15, Hebrews 4:7). It is a strong warning against unbelief. Yes, it made so many references to the Israelites rebellion of God during their time of testing in the desert. Because of that rebellion God declared, *"They shall never enter my rest"* (Hebrews 3:11). We are encouraged that we can enter His rest if, *"Today, we hear His voice and do not harden our hearts."* Today, we follow His lead; today, we follow His guidance. When we do not hear and follow, then we have rebelled against God, and will not find rest.

Today, I finally got it! Yes, I have heard His voice; yes, I have followed His instructions—almost. You see, I have always tried to work out in the natural what He has already declared to be so in the spiritual. There have been times that I have tried to map out the path when He has told me to go. We hear it said so many times; I have preached it. If He says go, you go and the way will be made. Now the really scary part is when I was trying to work it out or trying to think it out, I limited what God would do; I was rebelling against God. An unbelieving heart is a hardened heart. I do not care what you have done, or who you are. There is no rest for a hardened heart.

There remains, then a Sabbath-rest for the people of God: for anyone who enters God's rest also rest from his own work, just as God did from His. Let us therefore, make every effort to enter that rest, so that no one will fell by following their example of disobedience. For the word of

God is living and active. Sharper than any double-edged sword, it penetrates even to dividing soul and spirit, joints and marrow; it judged the thoughts and attitudes of the heart (Hebrews 4:9-12).

Sabbath is rest, peace. There indeed remains a rest, a place of peace for us when we do not rebel, when we do not harden our hearts. That rest allows us to rest as we are going through. No need to get to the beach, the lake, a porch, or the bed to rest. You can rest on your feet, rest through the storm, rest in spite of the chaos; you can rest. It sounds so simple, yet we get caught up often, trying to do it our way. We cannot do it our way; we have no idea how awesome that Sabbath rest is. Our way will not bring us peace. That is a hard lesson to learn. Oh, but it is so true.

It was never about my finding income, but about following God's will for my life. This has not been about my fortune or my misfortune, but about my journey and how I manage the challenges. Likewise, it is not about you or your misfortunes, it is about how you manage your journey. You have heard it before, without a test there is no strong testimony. How will you hold on during your period of trial? How will you survive? Oh, you will survive. I know you will, but you must let go of self in order to let God reshape you during this time. Be assured that your survival, your transformation does affect others.

As I try to finish this chapter, I am at my son's house. Great winds have passed through and knocked the power out in my neighborhood. Some Detroit areas have so many trees lining the streets and so many power cable that need updating that when strong winds or snows come, it causes problems with power. So for the third time this winter my power is out. I tried to continue writing but gave up and went to bed. Two hours later and the power was still out, it was beginning to get cold so I called my son. He had power at his house so I left to go there. About an hour after I arrived, the power went out at his house. Marq and my grandsons had been working on their music when I arrived. When the power went out, they did not stop but kept playing. I followed their lead and continued writing; after all, we still had daylight.

Can you see the difference? At my house when the power went out, I quickly gave up and went to bed. At my son's house, Marq and the boys continued their work, and that encouraged me to continue my work. We encountered the same problem, yet we handled it differently. On this journey, we need encouragement to continue by modeling, not necessarily with conversation. When I saw that they kept going, I kept going. We cannot give up, and we cannot give in so quickly. Oh, how quickly we give up when trials come. You see, the power will go out at times. It could be a test; it could be demonic influence. Whatever it is, get direction from God and continue as He directs. You may need to continue along the same path, you may need to switch paths; you may need to get still and mark time. Following only Holy Spirit's direction will bring you into a place of rest in God. After all, you are not making the decisions, but are being guided by the One who never makes a mistake. That alone sets anyone up for the *shalom*, the peace of God; everyone needs rest, everyone needs peace. We press on toward the mark of the high calling.

Occasionally that press is in standing still, but never is it in giving up. That was indeed a lesson for me today. Look at how God works!

I close with a word from a movie that was out a few years ago, *"Cool Runnings."* In the movie, the Jamaican bobsled team was asked what does *'Cool Runnings'* mean? Their reply is my blessing for you, "Peace be your journey."

References

Introduction

Encarta® World English Dictionary ©1999 Microsoft Corporation. All rights reserved. Developed for Microsoft by Bloomsbury Publishing Plc.

Tan, Siang-Tan. 2006. *Full Service: Moving from Self-Service Christianity to Total Servanthood.* Baker Books: Grand Rapids, MI.

Chapter 1

Fenelon, Francois. 1992. *The Seeking Heart.* Seed Sowers: Jacksonville, FL.

Pardue, Emily A. 2005. *The Drama of Dance in the Local Church.* Xulon Press: Longwood, FL.

Chapter 3

Fenelon, Francois. 1992. *The Seeking Heart.* Seed Sowers: Jacksonville, FL.

Chapter 4

Thompson, Millicent. 1995. *Don't Die in the Winter: Your Season Is Coming.* Treasure House.

Chapter 7

Merton, Thomas. 1961. *New Seeds of Contemplation*. New York: New Directions Publishing Corporation.

Chapter 9

Meyers, Nancy. *The Holiday*. Written, produced, and directed by Nancy Meyers. 136 min. Columbia Pictures and Universal Pictures. 2006. DVD.

Chapter 10

Nouwen, Henry J.M. 1979. *The Wounded Healer: Ministry in Contemporary Society.* New York: Image Books.

Sampson, Frederick III. Ashland Theological Seminary Fall Convocation 2003. Detroit.

Tan, Siang-Tan. 2006. *Full Service: Moving from Self-Service Christianity to Total Servanthood.* Baker Books: Grand Rapids, MI.

Chapter 11

Miller, Jim, Editor. *Men in Black*. Produced by Steven Spielberg, and directed by Barry Sonnenfeld. 98 minutes, Columbia Pictures. 1997. DVD

Chapter 17

Turteltaub, Jon. *Cool Runnings*. Directed by Jon Turteltaub. 98 minutes. Buena Vista Pictures. 1993. DVD.

About the Author

God's gifts to Rev. Dr. Emily A. Pardue have enabled her as a preacher, teacher, conference lecturer and speaker, locally, nationally, and internationally. As CEO of Write To Order, Ltd., she is a published author and playwright, director, and choreographer. A licensed, ordained Baptist minister, Dr. Pardue founded JAIA Sisters Ministries, Inc., in 2002. The ministry is a vehicle to assist believers in recognizing their spiritual giftedness and in utilizing those gifts individually and collectively for the advancement of God's kingdom.

God has used Dr. Pardue's creativity through writing, drama, and dance to render His Word in a distinct approach. Her theatrical work has been performed across the United States and Bahamas, in churches, schools, unions, and political arenas; and she has been called upon to lecture or teach in all of these arenas. Her first book, The Drama of Dance in the Local Church is of liturgical dance and the role it plays in the local church.

Dr. Pardue's focus is Spiritual Formation, freeing saints through Formational Counseling and equipping them for Spiritual Warfare. She has been an adjunct professor in Practical Theology at Ashland Theological Seminary, as well as advisor for Doctor of Ministry Students. She has studied and ministered in the Bahamas, Jerusalem, South Africa, and Oxford, England. She is certified as a mentor in Formational Counseling with the Institute of Formational Counseling in Ashland, OH.

Dr. Pardue received her Master of Divinity degree with honors and her Doctor of Ministry degree from Ashland Theological Seminary, where she also received the 2002 Spiritual Formation Award for the Detroit Campus.

Dr. Pardue offers individual Formational Prayers sessions as well as small groups in Formational Prayer, Spiritual Disciplines, and Spiritual Warfare. Visit her website, www.jaiasistersministries.org, for more information.

Contact Information

The author is available for book signings, workshops, seminars, retreats, and other speaking opportunities.

Send an email to:

revladyem@yahoo.com

Join her on Twitter at:

http://www.twitter.com/epardue

Join her on Facebook at:

http://www.facebook.com/emily.pardue

For information on ordering copies of *Notes from a Desert Place*, please contact the author or Kingdom Living Publishing:

Kingdom Living Publishing
P.O. Box 660
Accokeek, Maryland 20607
publish@kingdomlivingbooks.com
(301) 292-9010